What Are
Deserts?

by Lisa Trumbauer

Consulting Editor: Gail Saunders-Smith, Ph.D.

Consultant: Sandra Mather, Ph.D., Professor Emerita,
Department of Geology and Astronomy,
West Chester University
West Chester, Pennsylvania

Pebble Books

an imprint of Capstone Press
Mankato, Minnesota

Pebble Books are published by Capstone Press
151 Good Counsel Drive, P.O. Box 669, Mankato, Minnesota 56002
http://www.capstone-press.com

1 2 3 4 5 6 07 06 05 04 03 02

Library of Congress Cataloging-in-Publication Data
Trumbauer, Lisa, 1963–
    What are deserts? / by Lisa Trumbauer.
    p. cm.—(Earth features)
    ISBN 0-7368-0987-2
    1. Deserts—Juvenile literature. [1. Deserts.] I. Title. II. Series.
GB611 .T78 2002
551.41′5—dc21
                                                                2001000266

Summary: Simple text and photographs introduce deserts and their features.

Note to Parents and Teachers

The Earth Features series supports national science standards for units on landforms of the earth. The series also supports geography standards for using maps and other geographic representations. This book describes and illustrates deserts. The photographs support early readers in understanding the text. The repetition of words and phrases helps early readers learn new words. This book also introduces early readers to subject-specific vocabulary words, which are defined in the Words to Know section. Early readers may need assistance to read some words and to use the Table of Contents, Words to Know, Read More, Internet Sites, and Index/Word List sections of the book.

Table of Contents

A desert is dry land.
Very little rain falls
in a desert.

Most deserts are very hot. Some deserts can be very cold during winter. Snow may fall.

Some plants and animals
live in deserts. They do
not need much water
to live.

saguaro cactuses and fennec foxes

An oasis is an area of a desert that has water. An oasis can have green plants and pools of water.

Some deserts are sandy.

Wind moves the sand
to form dunes.

Some deserts are rocky.

Wind wears away
the rocks to form
many shapes.

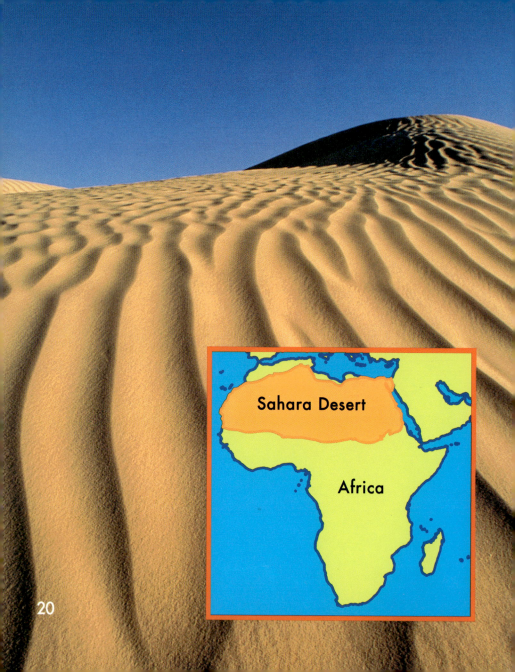

Sahara Desert

Africa

The Sahara Desert
is in northern Africa.
The Sahara Desert
is the largest desert
in the world.

Words to Know

dune—a hill of sand formed by the wind

oasis—a place in a desert where there is water; plants grow in an oasis; animals visit an oasis to drink water.

rain—water that falls in drops from clouds; deserts receive less than 10 inches (25 centimeters) of rain each year.

rocky—covered with rocks or stones

sandy—covered with sand; sand is tiny grains of rock that make up deserts or beaches.

snow—crystals of ice; snow falls from clouds.

wear away—to destroy something slowly; wind slowly wears away rocks to form new shapes.

wind—moving air

Read More

Fowler, Allan. *Living in a Desert.* Rookie Read-about Geography. New York: Children's Press, 2000.

Gray, Susan Heinrichs. *Deserts.* First Reports. Minneapolis: Compass Point Books, 2001.

Steele, Christy. *Deserts.* Biomes. Austin, Texas: Raintree Steck-Vaughn, 2001.

Wilkins, Sally. *Deserts.* Bridgestone Science Library: Ecosystems. Mankato, Minn.: Bridgestone Books, 2001.

Internet Sites

Desert Animal Printouts
http://www.zoomschool.com/coloring/desert.shtml

Nature Explorer—Life in the Desert
http://www.natureexplorer.com/LD/LD1.html

On the Line—Deserts
http://www.ontheline.org.uk/explore/nature/deserts/deserts.htm

Index/Word List

Word Count: 105
Early-Intervention Level: 14

Editorial Credits

Martha E. H. Rustad, editor; Kia Bielke, cover designer and illustrator;
   Kimberly Danger, photo researcher

Photo Credits

Comstock, Inc., cover, 1, 8, 16
CORBIS, 4, 12, 14, 18
Corel, 8 (inset)
International Stock/Roberto Arakaki, 10
Photo Network/Gene R. Russell, 6
Telegraph Colour Library/FPG International LLC, 20